JIM MORRISON

MY EYES HAVE SEEN YOU

JIM MORRISON

MY EYES HAVE SEEN YOU

Jerry Prochnicky
and
Joe Russo

AM Graphics & Printing
San Marcos, California

ISBN: 0-9651481-9-X

Library of Congress Catalog Card Number: 96-92143

First Edition, June 1996

Printed in the United States of America

AM GRAPHICS & PRINTING
San Marcos, CA

Jerry Prochnicky, dedication to: Stephanie Ann

Joe Russo, dedication to: Paul Rothchild (1935-1995)
for his friendship, encouragement and immeasurable
contribution to The Doors legacy.

Behind Jim Morrison

This book would not have been possible without the love and support
of my mother and father, Anna and Ivan Prochnickyj. Thank you to all of the
photographers/photo agencies that contributed their images, especially
Ethan Russell for the front and back covers that sets the stage. Thanks to
George Rodriguez for the great Whisky photos inside and writer/director
Dick Blackburn for the unique UCLA caricature drawing. And a special
gratitude to Frank Lisciandro for his words of wisdom through the years.
For keeping Morrison's spirit alive, a thank you to Kerry Humpherys of the
Doors Collectors Magazine in America and Rainer Moddemann of the
Doors Quarterly Magazine in West Germany. To special friends of the music;
David Causer, Pudge Diaczenko, Marianna Kris, Virginia Lohle, "Magic,"
Erica Meek, Jessica Meek, and Suzanne Regan. For all the fans in the
United States and worldwide who still believe in Jim Morrison. And finally to
The Doors — Ray Manzarek, Robbie Krieger and John Densmore for the music
that sounds like no other and that still exerts that voodoo magic.

A Peek Through The Lens

The shutter clicks capturing the image: Landscapes from Melbourne to Albuquerque to Alexandria; "There's no authority on film;" Meeting on the beach; There are things that are known and things that are unknown, in between are doors; Maced in New Haven; Leather Frankenstein; Numbing solace of alcohol; "The culmination, in a way, of our mass performing career;" The release of poetics; Paris blues; "Last words, last words … out;" Renew my subscription to the Resurrection; Mr. Mojo Risin'

Jim Morrison. The mere mention of the name conjures up a myriad of images, and The Doors — and what they stood for — remain something different for everyone. Without question, Jim Morrison is the quintessential rock idol. His death has come to be more significant than the presence of most rock starts today, and he is still able to exert an enormous pull, a mysterious force. His legacy is an ongoing, living record rather than a moment in history frozen forever in the past. These photos bring him back to life for a brief spell, illuminating the meaning of his demise and the possibility of what could have been. And the photographs lend a resonance to The Doors music which continues to enthrall three decades of rock fans with a sound that remains as powerful and profound in the '90s as it was in the '60s.

The sixties pulsed with the music that moved the consciousness of a whole generation. Everyone was plugged into what was going on. Not only was Morrison a manifestation of the time, but also an influence, amplifying the idea of artistic self-expression. And rock photography was at the cutting edge to the music scene. Still so young as an art form, rock photography was an act of creativity in itself and not just a standard collection of publicity stills. The photographers had a style and perspective all their own with the freedom to make and break the rules, and as a result the images were spontaneously created, exuding an essence of magic and mystery. They were there to capture a moment in time that would not only last a fraction of a second, but be preserved for a lifetime.

For a combined period of over five years, we have contacted dozens of private and obscure sources searching for rare photos of Morrison in all of his roles, from pedestrian hack to visionary genius. Photographers from four different countries have consented to allow their photographs to appear for the first time in this volume, capturing Morrison in many different settings, both public and private. These stark black and white images, sometimes in pure color, tell a story and reveal a truth. His life was like a movie — a subtle fantasy in which he was both hero and villain. The photos within this collection transcend the elusive myth of Jim Morrison, and they invite us to see beyond the image.

We felt that we knew him and this book is a look at someone whose life and times have shaped our own. It has taken us thirty years to realize that we will never see another like him again. This is our attempt to enlarge, make definitive, put into focus the memory of Jim Morrison with new photos. For old fans who remember and new ones who will discover the real Jim Morrison, we have created a visual biography, and not just your greatest hits compilation photobook. We tried to pace it like a Doors set with highs and lows so you'll have an emotional experience. The photos are a bridge to the past and a doorway to the future. Live with them. Learn from them. Such is the hope.

Jerry Prochnicky and Joe Russo

There are images I need to

complete my own reality...

Jim Morrison

James Morrison
Graduating Class of 1961
George Washington High School
Alexandria, Virginia

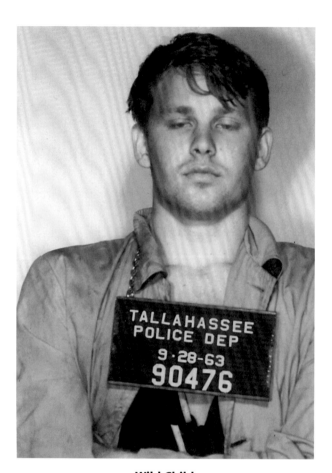

Wild Child
Disturbing the peace by being drunk, petty larceny of
Police Equipment, specifically umbrella and riot helmet.

First time on the theater stage at Florida State University
in the one-act drama, "The Dumb Waiter."

Captain George S. Morrison and his son James look out

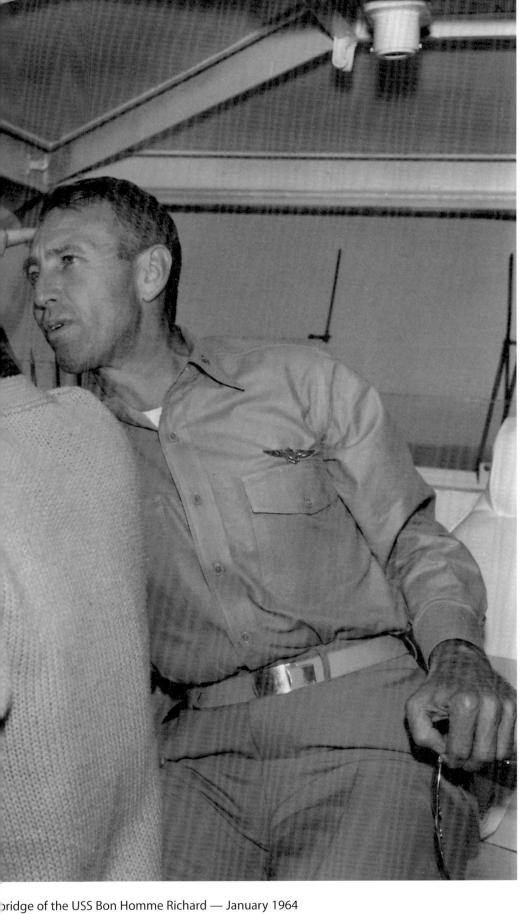

bridge of the USS Bon Homme Richard — January 1964

The Doors ruled Los Angeles

"An Hour For Magic"

Jamming with Van Morrison and Them, onstage at the Whisky a Go Go — June 1966

"Ride the snake" nights at the Whisky

November 1966 — Backstage at Ondine, a small rock and roll club in mid-town New York City

Working out on the tiny bandstand at Ondine

"A Feast of Friends"

Breaking on through at the Whisky a Go Go — May 16-21, 1967

Performing a three week stand at The Scene, a rock cellar off Times Square — June 1967

Genius of The Doors — made rock music around poetry

Caught up in the psychic web of the music

The Student Activities Board of The State University of New York
at Stony Brook in conjunction with Elektra Records presents:

LET EACH BECOME ALL HE IS CAPABLE OF BEING

a dance concert.

Music: The Doors and Tim Buckley

The Electric Shaman

SMILE

Absolutely Live at Danbury High School

Opening the doors in your mind

Hunter College — New York

Not so long ago, when rock 'n' roll was *dangerous* …

Krieger, Manzarek, Densmore in New Haven, Connecticut

Morrison, right after being maced backstage in the town of New Haven

"We weren't doing anything, you know, just standing there and talking…"

"This little man, in a little blue suit and a little blue cap…"

Busted onstage in New Haven for "breaching the peace" — December 9, 1967

The Lizard King

Ladies and gentle

Los Angeles, California … THE DOORS!

"WAKE UP!"

Something sinister, yet intelligent …
	Something not exactly evil, but very dark.

At the Kaleidoscope, The Doors world was the endless night

Touch Me

The single, most hypnotic figure in rock in the '60s

Bringing poetic drama to the stage at Westbury Music Fair, Long Island, New York — April, 1968

Waiting for Morrison

Admiral George Stephen Morrison

A poet's swagger, an outlaw's truth, and an artist's dedication

Setting the night on fire in Canada

Morrison walked a tightrope between hedonism and self-fulfillment

Tension and waiting for The Doors ou

c Hall in Cleveland on August 3, 1968

Everyday is a c

day is a drama.

First stop of their September 1968 Eur

at The Roundhouse in London

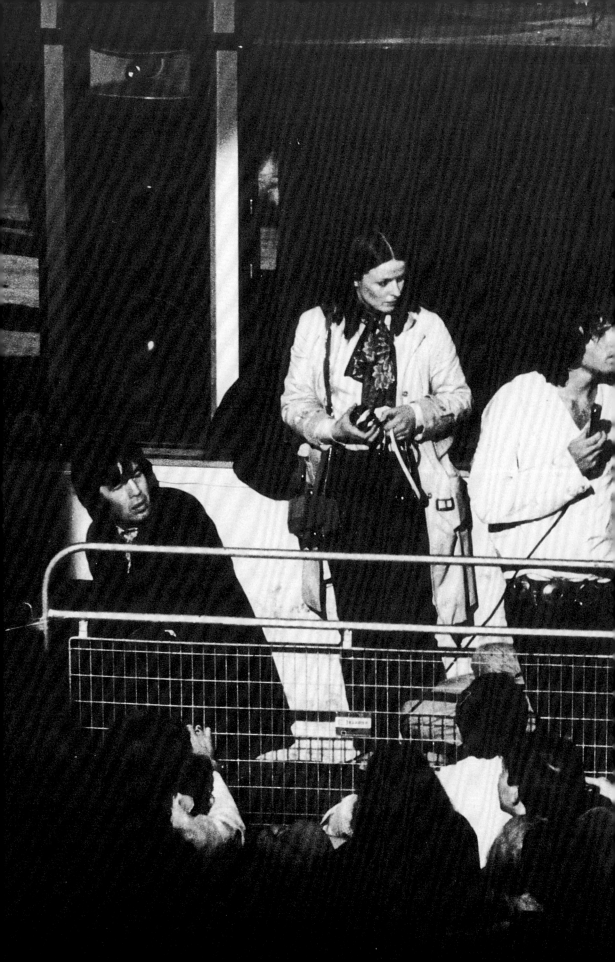

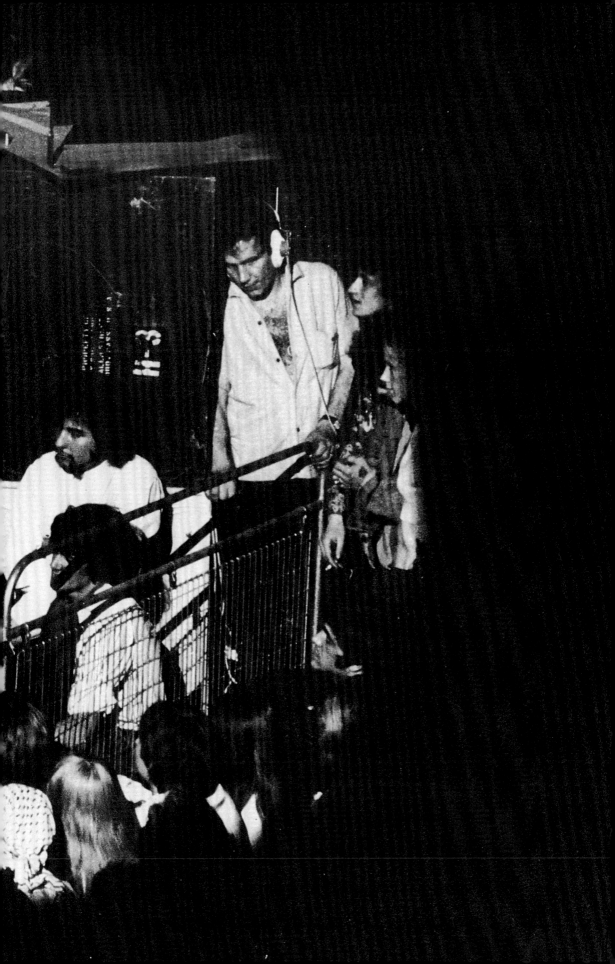

Taping for German TV in front of Town Hall

Jim Morrison giving his autograph to a female fan

Group's first concert in Frankfurt, Germany — September 14, 1968

Jim Morrison with Phoenix TV and radio personality, Pat McMahon

From a struggling bar band beginni

0,000 sellout at Madison Square Garden — January, 1969

March 1, 1969
Morrison in Miami. "THERE ARE NO RULES…"

Bozo Dionysus

April, 1969 — Jim Morrison with attorney Max Fink, arrives at the Los Angeles Federal Building
to fight extradition to Florida, in the aftermath of the Miami exhibition.

After three months of self exile, back on the road again in Chicago

July 1969 — Aquarius Theater, Los Angeles. Morrison was still capable of producing the goods onstage after the highly publicized Miami concert.

"People are strange" at Themis

My Wild Love, Pamela Susan

"Shhh. Now is that any way to behave at a rock 'n' roll concert?"

"That's New York for you. The only people that rush the stage are guys."

Buddha

The Establishment wanted to put Morrison away for good.

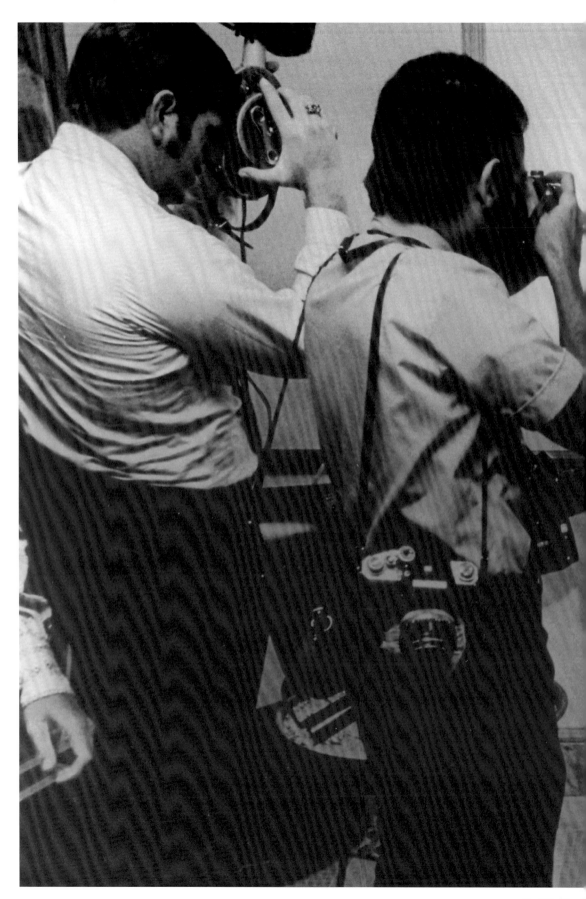

ency or Free Speech?

Hangin' out with close friend Babe Hill during a break in the proceedings

"I had a very unrealistic school boy attitude about the American judicial system."

Guilty of indecent exposure, but innocent of doing it in an obscene or suggestive manner?

ve Her Madly

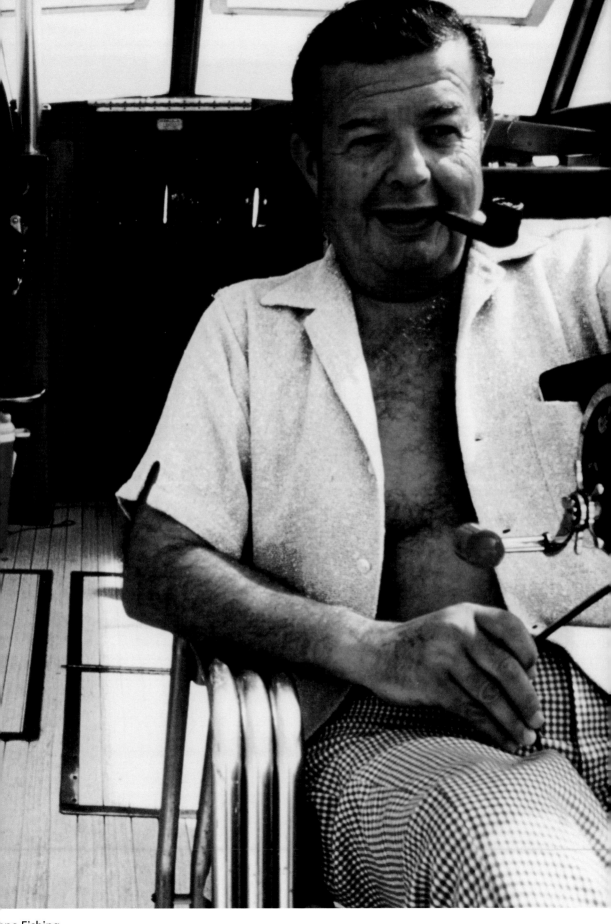

Gone Fishing

Recording poetry on the ni

mber 8, 1970, his 27th birthday

The <u>last</u> Doors concert with Morrison — December 12, 1970, New Orleans

The Doors recording *L.A. Woman* with Jerry Scheff (bas

Benno (rhythm guitar) at their funky sound studio

L.A. WOMAN

"Wounded Jim"

"The women are great & the food is gorgeous."

Riding Out The Final Storm
Paris — May 1971

STEFANO
27-6-1992
CHUS
ESPAÑA
DOBROSIA
This is the end
My only friend Jim
Awake from the
Severed Garden
ONLY THE
GOOD DIE YOUNG
Ride the Snake
ANDREA
MAURO
ALBE
HI! JIM
RENE
JIM

STONED IMMACULATE

A door opens on Morrison as a Poet

Resurrection

January 1993 — The Doors induction into the Rock 'n' Roll Hall of Fame.
Accepting on behalf of Jim is his sister, Anne Morrison.

Mr. Mojo Risin'

Photo Credits

Photo Credits (cont.)

Joe Sia

Joe Sia's first published photo was the cover of Rolling Stone (#41). His initial assignment was the original Woodstock. His first book *WOODSTOCK '69: A Photo Essay* sold a quarter of a million copies. Since then his photos have been published worldwide in hundreds of magazines and books, appearing in all forms of printed media (including newspapers, albums, CD's, posters, calendars, advertisements) as well as in TV specials, TV commercials, videos, and CD-ROMs. Joe's photos have also been used for murals. He has had his own one man exhibit: *Woodstock and the Summer of '69.* His photos have appeared in many other exhibits including the Jimi Hendrix Exhibits, Smithsonian Institute, and the Rock and Roll Hall of Fame.

If you are interested in purchasing any photos from this book or any of Joe's other photos (over 1,000 bands from 1969 to present). You can contact him at (203) 336-9221 or fax him at (203) 332-1658. You can also send a S.A.S.E. to him at his business address.

Joe Sia
PHOTOGRAPHER
955 Tunxis Hill Road
Fairfield, CT 06432
USA

The Authors

Jerry Prochnicky was touched and changed by rock music during the '60s especially the words and music of The Doors. This began a continuous and vivid emotional connection with Jim Morrison which culminated in being co-author of *BREAK ON THROUGH: The Life and Death of Jim Morrison* (William Morrow, 1991. Quill, 1992. Tokyo Shoseki, 1994). The New York Times ranks it as "the most objective, thorough and professional Morrison biography yet."

Performer-writer-musician — Joe Russo has been fronting the internationally renowned New York-based Doors tribute band *The Soft Parade* since 1990. He is currently collaborating with former Rascals drummer, Dino Danelli, on an original recording project. This is his second book.

Mail Order Information

For additional copies or as a gift to a friend send $23,
(outside USA $28) postpaid in U.S. Funds to:

Jerry Prochnicky
1611-A South Melrose Dr. #121
Vista, CA 92083
USA

Tell All The People

First set is over. Second Doors set with 100 more
<u>new</u> photos is scheduled for a later date.
MY EYES HAVE SEEN YOU … again.